it's the **XMAS**
FOOTBALL
QUIZ BOOK, JOKE BOOK, FACT BOOK

Publisher Information

Candescent Press

www.candescentpress.co.uk

info@candescentpress.co.uk

This book is an unofficial publication and is not authorised in any way by any of the football clubs mentioned. The information is vaguely accurate - but who knows these days? If you find something that is so wrong it makes your blood boil more than an incorrectly given penalty in the 87th minute, then send us a message!

Welcome to the Xmas Football Quiz Book, Joke Book, Fact Book.

We had a lot of fun putting together this book so we really hope you enjoy it too.

Given that the book is full of jokes, and tales of games which inevitably involved losers, we're bound to have offended your team or country somewhere. If we haven't, we're very sorry and will try and rectify it when we write a sequel.

The writers are based in England so when we refer to The Premier League or the top division we mean the English ones. Sorry Scotland and Wales, and the rest of the world (but you are included too!).

Pat yourself on the back!

We donate a large part of our profits on each book to charity - so thanks for buying the book (or go and give the person who bought it a big hug!).

So far we've helped charities working in the areas of Mental Health, Homelessness, Dementia and more. We'll keep going till people stop buying our books, so if you liked the book and want to help, a review would be appreciated!

Contents

it's the XMAS FOOTBALL

QUIZ BOOK, JOKE BOOK, FACT BOOK

Please Stop Singing Now

A quiz about songs that should mostly have never been recorded

When it was released, Band Aid's 'Do They Know It's Christmas?' was the biggest selling record in the UK charts of all time. Tony Hadley of Spandau Ballet sang on it. A totally different Tony Hadley used to play for both Colchester and Southend United. Coincidence? We don't think so!

Which, in a roundabout way, means it's time for a quiz about footballers singing...

1. Which of these was not a hit for Gazza? 'Fog on the Tyne', 'Howay the Lads' or 'Geordie Boys'?

2. Which duo known for their classic 80s haircuts (to be fair they did have them in the 80s) caused much pain to our ears with 'Diamond Lights'?

3. Andy (Andrew) Cole didn't trouble the charts with his biggest hit. Was it called Amazing, Outstanding, or Fabulous?

4. This footballer turned movie 'star', who made his big screen debut in Lock, Stock and Two Smoking Barrels, released a cover of the song 'Big Bad Leroy Brown'. Who was he?

5. Which German superstar - who played against England in the 1966 World Cup Final, and was known as Der Kaiser – once sang 'Gute Freunde Kann Niemand Trennen'? Was it Gerd Müller or Franz Beckenbauer?

6. Which national side tempted fate by calling their 1974 World Cup song 'Back Home'? England, Wales, or Northern Ireland?

7. According to Spurs, whose 'dream' was it to reach Wembley in 1981?

8. Which British national side sang 'Easy, Easy' in 1974? A clue? Their opponents have probably been singing it back to them ever since.

9. Two comedians and a singer from the Lightning Seeds combined for the song 'Three Lions' in 1996 (and again in 1998 and again in 2010!). You can have an imaginary point for each one you can name.

10. Lukas Podolski spent eleven weeks in the German top 100 with the single 'Halleluja'. True or False?

Answers on page 82

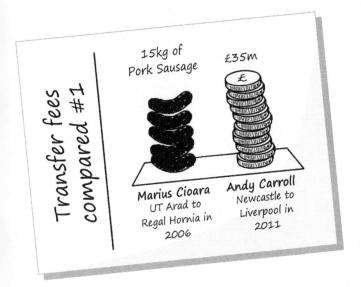

Transfer fees compared #1

15kg of Pork Sausage

£35m

Marius Cioara
UT Arad to Regal Hornia in 2006

Andy Carroll
Newcastle to Liverpool in 2011

Name that Football Club #1

Find the answer at the bottom of page 6.

Well I Never Did Know That!

Here are some facts that are Christmas related and are about football too. So take them down the pub and bore your mates!

The last time an English league match was due to be played on Christmas day was in 1983. Brentford planned to play Wimbledon - hoping that more fans would turn up. Brentford justified the move by explaining that "The men would go to the game, while their wives cooked the turkey". The fans were indeed enthused - but only to complain loudly - and so the match was moved to Christmas Eve.

Wimbledon won 4-3 in case you're wondering.

Jimmy Greaves scored four goals on Xmas day 1957, playing for Chelsea against Portsmouth. He hadn't played for the previous six weeks as his manager had been worried he was doing too well, and was getting too big for his boots!

Stoke and Bury played each other on Xmas Day 1954 - with Stoke winning 3-2. They then played the return fixture on Boxing Day (a draw), followed by an FA Cup 3rd round match in early January. And a replay on the 12th January. And another replay on the 17th. One more on the 19th. and a final replay on the 24th - with Stoke again winning 3-2. That's 7 matches between the same opponents in just one month.

Stoke's reward for winning was a match against Swansea in the 4th round, just five days later.

They lost.

Man City fans were overjoyed when Kiki Musampa joined on loan from Atlético Madrid. Ok, maybe not overjoyed, but this was before they became billionaires and beggars can't be choosers.

The really exciting news was still to come, when it was reported that Kiki's festively named brother Kris would be joining him (that's right... Kris Musampa).

Name That Club #1: Blackburn Rovers

It was of course a joke, but the internet being the way it is, the story had already been picked up by the UK tabloids, and before long it was cropping up in papers throughout the world.*

*or was it? We've searched and searched and we can only find the story on football forums. It may have been wiped from the memory of many news outlets, but we wonder if the 'successful hoax' is itself a hoax! If you know differently, drop us an email.

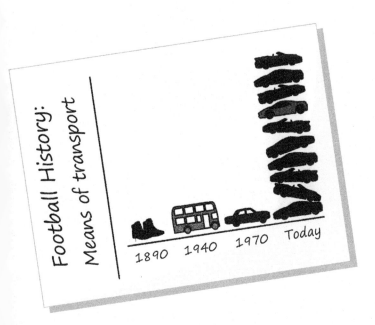

Football History:
Means of transport

1890   1940   1970   Today

Who's that Player?!

Look at the pictures and guess the name of the Christmassy player - simple!

Answer at the bottom of page 10

It's a Cracker!

Some bad jokes that are about Football - Like you get in Crackers at Christmas

Why did the footballer cross the road?

He was marking the chicken.

A rubbish football team is like an old bra...

It's got no cups and little support.

An Englishman, an Irishman, and a Scotsman walk into a bar.

The barman says: "Can you come back in 90 minutes lads? We're just watching the football".

It's a Festive Spot the Difference - Hooray!

A Ronaldo Wonderland

There are nine differences between the pictures on this page and the next - find them all, and give yourself an extra present!

Who's that Player? Roque Santa Cruz (Rocky Santa Cruise)

It's a Festive Spot the Difference - Hooray!

a Ronaldo Wonderland

See page 108 for the answers.

Happy Birthday Jairzinho-ho-ho

He was born on Christmas Dayyyyyyyy!

Born on 25th December 1944, Jairzinho is almost certainly the greatest of our Christmas Day footballers.

Born in Rio de Janeiro, he spent most of his career with his local team Botafogo, playing more than 400 times as a winger.

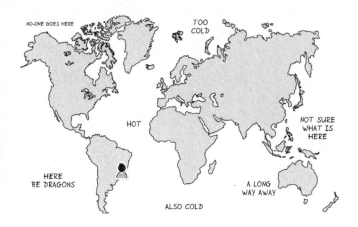

NO-ONE GOES HERE

TOO COLD

HOT

NOT SURE WHAT IS HERE

HERE BE DRAGONS

A LONG WAY AWAY

ALSO COLD

He played at three World Cups between 1966 and 1974, but it was at the 1970 tournament in Mexico that he truly joined the ranks of the greats.

Scoring seven goals, he helped Brazil become the first team to win the title three times - allowing them to take the trophy home for good. Unfortunately it was stolen in 1983 and is believed to have been melted down!*

Seven goals would have been enough to take home the Golden Boot in eight of the last nine World Cups - however in 1970 Gerd Müller scored ten, even though his team, West Germany, didn't reach the final.

*Please don't try this with your own Sunday League trophies as they are less likely to be made of solid gold.

Fact File

Full name: Jair Ventura Filho

Known as: Jairzinho

Nationality: Brazilian

International Caps: 81

International Goals: 33

Greatest Achievement: Scoring 7 goals on the way to winning the 1970 World Cup.

Last heard of: Managing Brazilian lower league side Esprof Atlético de Futebol e Clube.

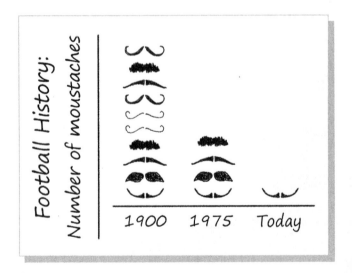

How Many?

A quiz about stadiums and stuff like that

Domestic women's football wasn't always played in front of crowds that would comfortably fit inside your local corner shop. During the First World War, women's football was as popular as turkey at Xmas. On Christmas Day 1917 the unusually named Dick, Kerr's (a works' team from Preston - and yes, they do have a comma slap, bang in the middle of their name!) beat Arundel Coulthard Factory in a charity match at Deepdale, in front of 10,000 people. 10,000? That's nothing you say - well, it was only just the beginning, and on Boxing Day 1920, a whopping 53,000 turned up to see Dick, Kerr's play St Helen's Ladies at Goodison Park. Another

14,000 couldn't even get inside! The FA duly took note and banned women from playing at their members' grounds. Why? Because women weren't physically capable of course! Good to know the FA isn't still run by such foolish types.

Anyway - that's a roundabout way of getting to the quiz about Big crowds and Big stadiums!

1. Manchester United's record attendance was 83,260 in a game against Arsenal in 1948. Where was the match played?

2. Prior to their move to the Olympic Stadium, West Ham United's biggest home gate (42,322 against Spurs in 1970) was at the ground many of us know as Upton Park. What was its official name?

3. We've seen that women's football has been played in front of some big crowds in the past - but the record Goodison Park gate was actually broken in 2012, when Britain beat which team 1-0 in the Olympics? Brazil, Argentina, or Canada?

4. Hampden Park is one of the biggest football grounds in the country, with a capacity of over 52,000. Which club team play their home games there?

5. Which Brazilian stadium holds the record for the highest ever football attendance – a whopping 199,854? The Macaroon or Maracanã Stadium

6. Bolton Wanderers played Manchester City in front of nearly seventy thousand fans·in a 1933 FA Cup match. What was the name of Bolton's ground in 1933? Smokehouse Lane, Burnden Park or Wanderers' Alley?

7. The largest stadium in world football in 2014 is the Rungnado May Day Stadium. Its capacity is 150,000 and a clue to its location is that attendances are often exactly 150,000. Which country is it in? China, North Korea or India?

8. Only one of the five largest football stadiums in the world is in Europe. Whose stadium is it, and what is it called?

9. With a capacity of 120,000 Salt Lake Stadium is one of the largest in world football. Which country is it located in?

10. The Millennium stadium is Wales' largest football ground. Is its capacity 74,500, 79,500 or 84,500?

Answers on page 84

Xmas 1st Eleven

A rather unbalanced team made up of footballers with amusingly Christmassy names

What is it with footballers and Christmassy names? There's obviously something weird going on because our first eleven has five strikers up front - and that's after we've converted Noel Whelan and Andy Carroll into a 'formidable' central defensive partnership! We even had to pretend we couldn't spell to get a goalkeeper!

Manager:
KEVIN Keegan*

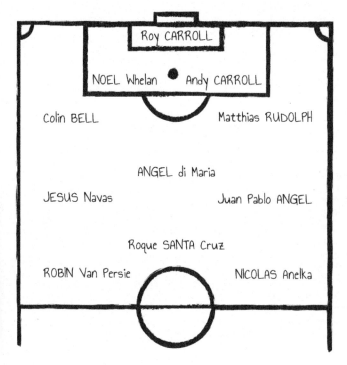

Roy CARROLL

NOEL Whelan • Andy CARROLL

Colin BELL   Matthias RUDOLPH

ANGEL di Maria

JESUS Navas   Juan Pablo ANGEL

Roque SANTA Cruz

ROBIN Van Persie   NICOLAS Anelka

*What do you mean, you can't see the connection? Home Alone! Christmas classic! Kevin McAllister! Now - Hang your head in shame.

Pulling Crackers

Some more bad jokes that are about Football

Player: "Boss - I've just had a great idea for improving the team."

Manager: "Fantastic! When are you leaving?"

How can you tell if there's a footballer hiding in your fridge?

There are stud marks in the butter.

How many footballers does it take to change a light bulb?

Four. One to change the bulb and three to help with the post-change celebration.

Name that Football Club #2

Find the answer at the bottom of the next page.

Mixed up Stadiums - Anagrams #1

We've mixed up the letters in the names of some famous (and not so famous) football stadiums. Can you work them out?

An extra point for naming the team that plays at each stadium.

1. Drank Hemp Pa

2. Dim Bard Forgets

3. Elf And I

4. Lava Perk

5. Dangerous Reoccur

6. Alan Adds A Mixture

7. Shy Heat

8. Work Us Dynamite

9. Sparkler Huts

You can find the answers on page 102

Name That Club #2: Fulham

Goals, Goals, and more Goals

A quiz about people scoring lots and lots of goals

The most goals scored in an English league game took place at Christmas 1935.

Oldham Athletic were on the wrong end of a 13-4 scoreline as they were thrashed by Tranmere Rovers on Boxing Day. The game was in the Third Division North - from those times when travelling 100 miles was just for the big boys (like Huddersfield and Brentford). That's 17 (seventeen) goals in 90 minutes, or one goal every 5.294118 minutes.

So, to celebrate this momentous match we've got a quiz about scoring lots of goals...

1. On 11th April 2001, American Samoa were beaten 31-0 in a World Cup qualifying match. Which team beat them? Australia, New Zealand or Papua New Guinea?

2. Two teams with bulging trophy cabinets met in the very first Full Members Cup final in 1986. At the time neither had won a trophy in a decade, but a shiny cup was at stake that day, and a thrilling match ended 5-4. Which teams played in the final? (Clue: They've both won a lot since!)

3. On 12th September 1885, Dundee Harp beat Aberdeen Rovers 35-0 in the Scottish Cup. It would have been a world record; however on the very same day another Scottish Cup game ended 36-0! Who scored 36 goals? Arbroath, Celtic, or Hibernian?

4. Ipswich Town (in 1995) and Wigan (in 2009) have both conceded nine goals in Premier League Games. For a point each, name the teams that beat Ipswich and Wigan.

5. Poor Wigan improved the next season (2010) - only losing 8-0 to the eventual Champions. Who beat them this time?

6. One of the most astonishing World Cup matches took place in 1954 - when one nation, known for its skiing holidays, came back from 3-0 down to beat another nation, also known for its skiing holidays, 7-5. Name the two countries involved.

7. Which red team, a regular in Europe at the time, recorded their highest ever win (11-0) against Strømsgodset in the 1974 UEFA Cup Winners' Cup?

8. Alex Ferguson's last ever game for Manchester United was a high scoring draw against West Brom. Was the score 3-3, 4-4 or 5-5?

9. In a 1943 cup game, having lost the away leg 3-0, Real Madrid won the return 11-1. 70 years later it was still their record win. Who did they beat?

10. In 2002, a match in Madagascar ended with a world record 149-0 scoreline. How did the winning team score so many goals

Answers on page 86

Bang! It's a Cracker

Time for another dose of crackery fun!

How can you tell if Norwich City are losing?

Its five past three.

Why was Cinderella thrown off the football team?

She always ran away from the ball.

What's the difference between a triangle and Wigan?

A triangle has three points.

Happy Birthday
Gary McAllister

He was born on
Christmas Dayyyyyyyy!

Gary McAllister played at the top levels of British football for an impressive twenty years!

He was born in Motherwell, on Xmas Day 1964 and made his debut for his local team aged just 17! Shortly after making his debut, Jock Wallace took over as manager, and spotting

McAllister's potential, he pinned him against the wall and threatened "if you don't become Scotland captain one day, I'll kick your backside all over Lanarkshire". Fortunately he did become captain of his country so his backside was saved.

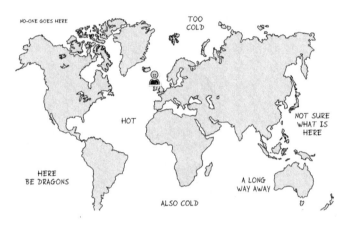

After leaving Motherwell he had a five year spell at Leicester City, mostly in the second tier, where he twice made the PFA team of the year. Success followed when he joined Leeds and helped lead them to a first top division title in nearly twenty years.

Two spells with Coventry were punctuated by a trophy laden couple of years at Liverpool. He was part of the squad that won a treble of trophies (FA Cup, League Cup and UEFA Cup) in 2001•

•or five trophies if you're a Liverpool fan - they also won the UEFA Super Cup and the Charity Shield.

Fact File

Full name: Gary McAllister

Known as: The Enforcer

Nationality: Scottish

International Caps: 57

International Goals: 5

Greatest Achievements: Helping Leeds win the English first division title, after a near twenty year wait.

Last heard of: Commentating on matches for BT Sport.

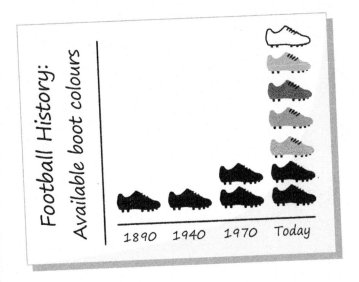

Match the player to the country

Draw a line between the player & the country they played for.

Ahmed Hassan   Ecuador

Mohamed Al-Deayea   Egypt

Claudio Suárez   Estonia

Iván Hurtado   Latvia

Iker Casillas   Mexico

Vitālijs Astafjevs   Saudi Arabia

Cobi Jones   Spain

Adnan Al-Talyani   United Arab Emirates

Martin Reim   United States

Answers on page 111

Name that Football Club #3

Find the answer at the bottom of the next page.

They Scored on Boxing Day!

66 goals were scored in just ten 1st division matches on 26th December 1963. Some of the scorers are named below. Can you find them? Look up, down, sideways, diagonally and backwards. Solution on page 106

```
T H I C B E G J Z P H M V M I
A T L I R E X Y G C P U I Y U
G I Q L Q A Y F R D X L B K L
G M P F A L W U A Z Y L W D V
E S F X V N H F Y E L E T A H
L W L M D C G J O S G R D O E
U O P V L P N I A R Q Y C I R
U R Z L J Y A K W W D L R R G
I R A F U D G E A N B U N R G
B A V E N A B L E S D N E J U
C A F U P A Z F F U V A D D X
H C K Y O O R Z G F V Q M Q M
E U J E C A R J O E X T I H Z
R W B B R V Y C S K R Z U H O
D E V S C L S B Z C X H G V R
```

ALLCHURCH, ARROWSMITH, BAKER, CRAWFORD, DURIE, FUDGE, GREAVES, HATELEY, HERD, LEGGAT, MULLERY, VENABLES, WIGNALL

Name That Club #3: Liverpool

Facts, Glorious Facts!

A story most of you will know, and some things you won't

By Xmas 1914 the First World War was just five months old. Much of the war was being fought in trenches less than the width of a football pitch apart, and as a result combatants on both sides would regularly engage in shouted conversation.

As Xmas approached, both sides began to talk of truces and taking a break from the killing. Informal meetings took place in No Man's Land (the space between the trenches), with conversations about the hardships of war, talk of home, and the exchange of cigarettes and food as gifts.

As Xmas approached talk would often turn to football, and many historians believe that informal football matches took place in a handful of locations across the front line. The likelihood is that these 'matches' were short kickabouts at best, and may well not have even been played with footballs! (Perhaps a tin of beans was used - which must have been even harder to control on the muddy ground).

As the war progressed, and the killing escalated, the goodwill on both sides fell away. Add in the fact that senior officers warned against future 'fraternisation', and it's not surprising that, sadly, the truces never happened in quite the same way again.

Although British teams haven't played on Xmas day for many years, it was common in the late 1800s. Teams would regularly play matches on both Xmas Day and Boxing Day. Due to poor public transport at Christmas, these games would often be local derbies, sometimes even back to back home and away games against the same team. Elsewhere in this book we've told you that Oldham were beaten by Tranmere 13-4 on Boxing Day 1935. They'd played on Christmas Day too, but amazingly, Oldham had won that game 4-1!

The Christmas Day match between Chelsea and Charlton Athletic in 1937 proved to be memorable for Charlton keeper Sam Bartram.

Heavy fog descended on to the pitch shortly after the start - and at one point the referee stopped the game till the fog cleared a little. Bartram could see his team were doing well, and as the fog slowly came back he saw almost nothing of the ball. Pleased that his team were on top in the game, he paced up and down his penalty area, and the minutes ticked by.

He was more than a little surprised when a policeman appeared out of the fog - walking across the pitch. The officer, with an astonished look on his face, shouted out: "What are you doing? - the match was called off fifteen minutes ago!"

You only sing when you're losing!

A quiz about losers - because everyone has to lose sometimes*

Four days before Christmas in 1957, Huddersfield Town scored a magnificent six goals. A wonderful pre-Christmas gift for all their fans, who had travelled half the length of England to watch them play Charlton Athletic.

Unfortunately, that day Charlton scored seven.

Without further ado - for all the glorious losers out there, a magnificent quiz...

*Free philosophy lesson.

1. It's 2004. You're playing at home, winning 3-0 at half time in an FA Cup tie. One of your opponent's best players gets sent off DURING the half time break for dissent. You lose 4-3 with the winning goal coming in the 90th minute. You are Spurs - but who were you playing?

2. Artmedia are from Slovakia and if you've heard of them, it's probably because you're a fan of the Scottish club they knocked out of the Champions League in 2005. Artmedia won their home leg 5-0 and then clung on to lose by just 4 goals in the away game, against which team?

3. Liverpool were the shock 1-0 losers in the 1988 FA Cup Final. Who beat them, and, for an extra imaginary point, which future Northern Ireland manager scored the winning goal?

4. France arrived at the 2002 World Cup Finals as World and European Champions. They incredibly lost their first match 1-0 to an African team that went on to reach the Quarter Finals? Name that team.

5. In 1966, Italy were beaten 1-0 in one of the biggest ever World Cup upsets. Italy, twice winners of the trophy, were playing an Asian team who had never previously qualified. Which country beat Italy?

6. When the Faroe Islands entered qualifying for the 1992 European Championships, they didn't even have a pitch to play on. Their first competitive game was played in Sweden against a team that once finished in third place at a World Cup Finals. The Faroe Islands won 1-0. Who were the big losers that day?

7. Germany don't often get beaten at home. And they would never let one of their biggest rivals score five goals against them in a competitive match - or would they? We all know England beat Germany 5-1 in 2001 - but who scored the goals?

8. Spain were hosting their first World Cup. Fancied to do well, they were leading their group going into the final game of the first stage. They were playing a country with a population just 1/25th the size of Spain. A country who hadn't qualified for over 20 years. They lost the game 1-0. Which team beat them, and who scored the winning goal?

9. We're back at the 2002 World Cup Finals and once again it's Italy on the end of a shock result. One of the unfancied host nations is playing - surely there can only be one result? Indeed there is, as the Italians lose 2-1 and typically conjure up a host of conspiracy theories. But which team beat them?

10. It's only the Capital One Cup - and they were playing a weakened team. But when the new manager of Manchester United is Louis Van Gaal, and he's spent more than a little cash, you don't expect to lose 4-0 to a team two divisions below. Which team beat United?

Answers on page 89

Transfer fees compared #2

Kenneth's body weight in shrimp

£1.18m - First million pound player

£

Kenneth Kristensen
Vindbjart to
Floey
in 2002

Trevor Francis
Birmingham to
Notts Forest
in 1979

Name that
Football Club #4

Find the answer at the bottom of page 42.

Mixed up Players - Anagrams #2

We've mixed up the letters in the names of some famous footballers. Can you unscramble them?

1. Reverts Danger

2. Hazel Six Canes

3. Peel

4. Leather Bag

5. I Tile A Ballroom

6. Err Ben Banjo

7. Towel Or Windbreaks

8. Ale Raindrop

9. Obey Or Bomb

You can find the answers on page 105.

Some Random Results

December 25th 2013

Division 1 (Tunisia)

They still play football on Christmas Day in Tunisia. Good for them!

US Monastirienne	0-0	Stade Gabésien
Stade Tunisien	2-0	ES Métlaoui
Grombalia Sport	2-1	JS Kairouanaise
Etoile du Sahel	1-0	Club Africain
ES Tunis	4-0	LPS Tozeur
EGS Gafsa	0-2	Hammam Lif
CA Bizertin	1-2	CS Sfaxien
AS Marsa	2-3	Olympique de Béja

Name That Club #4, Celtic

Some Less Random Results

December 25th 1957
English Division 1

The last time a full programme of top flight English games was played on Christmas Day.

Blackpool	5-1	Leicester City
Burnley	2-1	Manchester City
Chelsea	7-4	Portsmouth
Everton	1-1	Bolton Wanderers
Manchester United	3-0	Luton Town
Newcastle United	1-4	Nottingham Forest
Sheffield Wednesday	4-4	Preston North End

Name that
Football Club #5

Find the answer at the bottom of the page.46

They call him What?!

A quiz about some nicknames that footballer's have.

Ariel Ortega, the wonderfully skilful Argentinean, who played in three world cups, was nicknamed Burrito. He wasn't named after the tasty Mexican meal, but because Burrito translates as Little Donkey in Spanish.

Little Donkey is of course a Christmas Carol - and that's all the justification we need for another quiz!

1.   Which Italian, who played for Middlesbrough, was known as The White Feather?

2. Who Manchester United star was the Baby-Faced Assassin?

3. What was England goalkeeper David James' cowboy themed nickname?

4. Which alliterative Frenchman was known as Zizou?

5. Which ex-England manager was known as The Professor?

6. US footballer Eric Wynalda got his nickname because he liked to dress in striped tops and hide amongst similarly attired gentlemen (at least that's our theory). What was his nickname?

7. Javier Zanetti has played over 600 games for Inter, and picked up an unusual nickname along the way. Is he known as The Plough, The Tractor, or The Combine Harvester?

8. Why wouldn't you like Givanildo Vieira de Sousa when he's angry?

9. Spanish player Emilio Butragueño, was known as the Vampire. True or False?

10. Which of England's World Cup winning Charlton brothers was known as The Giraffe?

Answers on page 93

Name That Club #5, West Ham United

Xmas Comes Early

In 1966 England's Xmas present arrived in July when they won the World Cup. The team that started that day became household names, but can you name them, from just the vowels in their names?

1. _o_ _o_   _a_ _ _

2. _eo_ _e   _o_e_

3. _a_ _   _ _a_ _ _o_

4. _o_ _ _   _oo_e

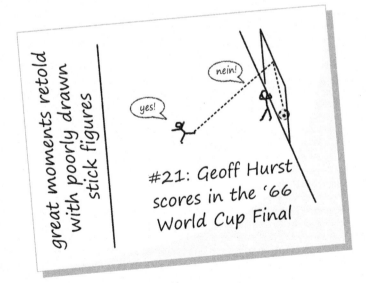

great moments retold with poorly drawn stick figures

yes!

nein!

#21: Geoff Hurst scores in the '66 World Cup Final

5. _a_   _i_ _o_

6. _o_ _ _   _ _i_e_

7. A_a_   _a_ _

8. _o_ _ _   _ _a_ _ _o_

9. _a_ _i_   _e_e_ _

10. _eo_ _   _u_ _ _

11. _o_e_   _u_ _

Answers on page 103 (Although there's a large clue to one of the answers "hidden" on this page.)

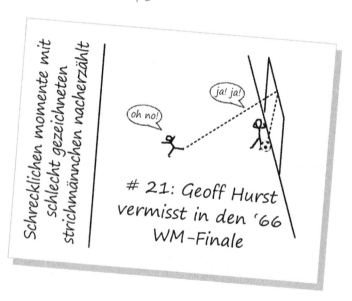

A Real Cracker

It was the annual Bugs v Spiders cup final. Everyone was very excited. The match kicked off and the spiders raced into an early lead. They scored goal after goal, and by half time were leading ten-nil.

At the start of the second half the Bugs took off their striker and brought on Cecil the Centipede. Cecil was everywhere - tackling in midfield, blocking shots, and scoring goals - in fact he was so good that the Bugs won the match eleven-ten.

The Spider's manager was confused. He asked the Bug's boss, "If he's so good, why didn't you play him from the start?"

"We'd have loved to", came the reply, "but it took him the whole first half just to put his boots on!"

Who's that Player?!

Look at the pictures and guess the name of the Christmassy player - simple!

Answer at the bottom of page 52

Cracker time!

Put down some plastic sheeting 'cos your sides are about to split.

Did you hear about the football match?

He played as a striker.

At least he did until he burnt out.

Two flies are playing football in a saucer.

'I hope we do better than this next week' says the first fly. '...we're playing in the cup!'

Why can't you get a cup of tea at Spurs ground?

Because all the mugs are on the field and all the cups are in Manchester.

Oh we do like to be beside the Seaside!

How much do you know about football clubs that play by the coast?

Brighton and Hove Albion's biggest ever attendance of 36,747 was at a Christmas game. They beat Fulham 3-0 on 27th December 1958.

Now most of you will know that Brighton and Hove just happen to be by the seaside (beside the sea). So here's a quiz about seaside teams...

Who's that Player? Robin Van Persie (Purse-E)

1. Blackpool is clearly the world's finest seaside town, so what better place to start. One of their nicknames is the colour of their shirts - What is it?

2. Alan Shearer scored a whopping 260 Premier League goals - but which seaside club did he start his professional career with?

3. Which Welsh coastal club play at the Liberty Stadium?

4. Barcelona are the only seaside team in this quiz who have won the European Cup - but when did they first win it - 1961, 1986 or 1992?

5. Bournemouth may not have a long list of European titles, but they did win the very first Football League Trophy (then known as the Associate Members' Cup) in 1983-84. Who did they beat in the final? Hull City, Burnley or Millwall?

6. They famously beat Liverpool with a shot that deflected off a Beach Ball. How seasidey is that? Name the team.

7. Which coastal club are known as the Shrimpers?

8. Which Scottish football club play in the Granite City?

9. Portsmouth won the 2008 FA Cup final - but who did they beat?

10. And an easy one to finish. Which coastal city has a club whose name ends in Argyle?

Answers on page 95

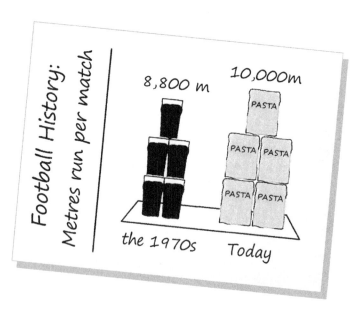

Football History:
Metres run per match

8,800 m

10,000m

the 1970s   Today

Happy Birthday
Emmanuel Amuneke

He was born on
Christmas Dayyyyyyyy!

What's so special about him? Well, for a start Emmanuel Amuneke was born on 25th December 1970 which makes him a star in our book.

His career wasn't quite as stellar as it could have been, due to a number of serious injuries, but he made the most of the games he played. He was a Nigerian international, and was part of their first ever World Cup Finals squad in 1994. He scored in games against Bulgaria and Italy, as Nigeria reached the knockout stages.

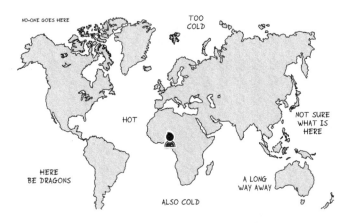

1994 was a big year for Amuneke as he was also part of the Nigeria team which won the African Cup of Nations, and he was later voted African Footballer of the Year. He beat George Weah into second place, which shows just how good he was!

As an overage player he won a gold medal at the 1996 Summer Olympics, beating Argentina in the finals, and he even played briefly for Barcelona before a serious injury stalled his career.

So, Santa hats off to this Festive Super Eagle!

Fact File

Full name: Emmanuel Amuneke

Nationality: Nigerian

International Caps: 27

International Goals: 9

Greatest Achievement: Winning African Footballer of the Year in 1994.

Last heard of: Coaching Ocean Boys of Nigeria in 2009.

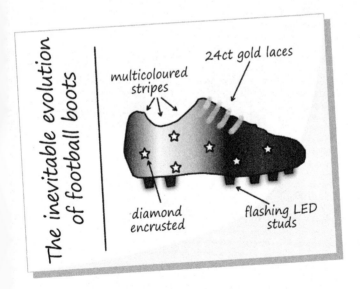

The inevitable evolution of football boots

24ct gold laces

multicoloured stripes

diamond encrusted

flashing LED studs

Name that Football Club #6

Find the answer at the bottom of page 60.

Mixed up Teams - Anagrams #3

We've mixed up the letters of nine football teams. Can you work out the proper team names?

1.   Honest Formatting

2.   Red Field Shutdown

3.   Raw Raw Horn Developments

4.   He Fled Sideways Fend

5.   Learn As

6.   Trump So Hot

7.   Rent Covers Roads

8.   Bunny Chimera

9.   Roughly Ply Team

You can find the answers on page 107.

Bad Crackers

Some Jokes that would probably get rejected by the Christmas Cracker Police.

My doctor told me to avoid any unnecessary excitement.

So I started supporting Fulham.

I was driving home from work yesterday when I saw a Newcastle United season ticket nailed to a tree.

I thought "I'm having that - a good nail always comes in handy"

Why don't you play football in the jungle?

There are too many cheetahs!

Name That Club #6: Southend United

Naughty or Nice?

Some footballers won't be on Santa's present list.

In 1936 Ambrose Brown travelled with Wrexham all the way to Hull for a Christmas Day fixture. We make that about 150 miles. Not only did his team lose, but he was sent off after just 20 seconds!

At the time it was the fastest ever sending off - and we're celebrating with a quiz about players that got on to Santa's naughty list.

1. Which fiery Italian was banned for 11 matches in 1998 for pushing over referee Paul Alcock?

2. Chelsea dumped Adrian Mutu in 2004 after he got in trouble with gambling, women, or drugs?

3. In the 2006 World Cup, English referee Graham Poll sent off Josip Šimunić for receiving more than one yellow card. What was unusual, and which team did Šimunić play for?

4. This Brazilian, bought by Inter as a teenager for over £10 million, must hold some kind of record for being thrown out of clubs. Amongst other incidents, Inter twice sent him back to Brazil on unpaid leave, São Paulo released him early from a loan after he wandered out of training, Roma terminated his 3 year contract after just seven months, and Corinthians released him due to an apparent lack of interest in training! Who is he?

5. Luis Suarez had a nibble of Giorgio Chiellini at the 2014 World Cup - but this wasn't the first time he'd snacked on an opponent, it was the third time! Which club was he playing for when he had his first footballer dinner?

6. Manchester United's Eric Cantona famously karate kicked an opposition fan who was abusing him. Which club was the fan supporting?

7. In 2014 Arsenal's Kieran Gibbs was sent off for handball in a match against Chelsea. What was unusual about his dismissal?

8. Maradona crushed England's World Cup hopes in 1986 when he handled the ball into the net. He later called it the 'hand of God' - but who was the England keeper that he tricked?

9. Norman Hunter was a classic hard man in that heyday of dodgy tackling, the late 60s/early 70s. But was his nickname Breaks Yer Back, Grinds Yer Gears, or Bites Yer Legs?

10. Zinedine Zidane would have been known simply as one of the greatest footballers ever - until he headbutted an opponent in his last ever game, the 2006 World Cup Final. Who did he headbut, and what team did his opponent play for?

Answers on page 97

Match the stadium to the team

Draw a line between the team & the stadium they play in.·

Hillsborough Stadium

Elland Road

Riverside Stadium

Ricoh Arena

Portman Road

Stadium of Light

Molineux

St Andrew's

Valley Parade

Birmingham City

Bradford City

Coventry City

Ipswich Town

Leeds United

Middlesbrough

Sheffield Wednesday

Sunderland

Wolverhampton Wanderers

Answers on page 109

·Assuming they haven't moved or aren't sponsored by the local takeaway, and have had to rename the stadium The Chip Butty Arena.

All I want for Xmas...

...is a Dukla Prague Away Kit

1986 was a big year for combined Football and Xmas events.

Yes - it was the year that Half Man, Half Biscuit released their EP 'The Trumpton Riots'. On the B-side, one of the greatest songs about football and Xmas* was hidden away: "All I want for Xmas is a Dukla Prague away kit".

As a special treat - we've recreated the kit and can't help but notice that its main feature appears to be Mickey Mouse frothing at the mouth. Still. Takes all sorts.

*Ok - maybe the only one - although there is a rumour that the 'You' in Maria Carey's hit single 'All I want for Xmas is You' is actually ex-Stoke City 'long throw expert' Rory Delap.

If your brain was as big as a football...

Here's a puzzle so hard that some of you might still be working it out NEXT Christmas!

Five of the world's best players are competing in the World Cup. Each player will reach a different stage in the competition, will travel to training in a different way, and plays in a different position. Follow the clues below to work out:

Which player will reach the Quarter Finals?

Who will travel by Bicycle?

Who plays as a Winger?

CLUES

1. Claudio Kicko doesn't drive a Ferrari.

2. Gary Boots will reach two stages further in the Cup than Joey Jump.

3. The footballer that plays in goal doesn't drive a Porsche.

4. The footballer with the Porsche will be knocked out before the player with the Ferrari.

5. The footballer that plays in Central Midfield will be knocked out three rounds before the player who drives the Porsche.

6. Gary Boots isn't a Goalkeeper.

7. Of the player who will reach the Semi Finals and the footballer that plays as a striker, one will walk to training and the other is Billy Ball.

8. Gary Boots will drive his Bentley to training.

9. Billy Ball doesn't play as a Winger.

If you've got a brain as big as Santa's belly then you can solve the puzzle in your head. If you're like us you might want to use the grid on the next page.

PUZZLE GRID: Put a tick in a box you know is true, and a cross in a box that can't be. So for clue 1, you'd put a cross where Claudio Kicko meets Ferrari, as Claudio Kicko doesn't drive a Ferrari. For clue 2, if Gary Boots play two rounds more than Joey Jump, you straight away know Gary can't be knocked out before the Quarter Finals, so put crosses where Gary meets Qualifying and Group. Remember, when you know something for sure, that also rules out other options. Use a pencil and have a rubber handy!

	Qualifying	Group	Qtr Final	Semi Final	Final	Goalkeeper	Right Back	Ctr Midfield	Winger	Striker	Ferrari	Bicycle	Bentley	Porsche	Walks
Gary Boots															
Claudio Kicko															
Billy Ball															
Joey Jump															
Goalinho															
Ferrari															
Bicycle															
Bentley															
Porsche															
Walks															
Goalkeeper															
Right Back															
Ctr Midfield															
Winger															
Striker															

See page 104 for the answers.

They played at Xmas

December 25th 1957

Find the names of all the first division teams that played the last time we had a full Xmas programme. Look up, down, sideways, diagonally and backwards. Solution on page 110

```
C U N V X D S L X A Q J A J N R
K B O L I V H O O R M C X O M W
R F T S R C E P Y O F Q T E N R
T F L E E V F E I V P U D O V C
O V O C T K F S P N L K T J D B
M M B J S F I O B G O T C E N C
A Q V B E L E W H U S T T A H M
N E E F C L L H Z F R I S E L H
C R H J I N D D O T N N L E O B
I E U K E Z W R D U Q S L U R E
T P Z P L N E V N Y E A M E F P
Y E Q W N S D A Z A F S S L Y W
U O B S T E M N E W C A S T L E
N O T R E V E U N K G J O D T E
H T U O M S T R O P L V E U G P
K O W N S V V L R T R I W W M Q
```

BLACKPOOL, BOLTON, BURNLEY, CHELSEA, EVERTON, LEICESTER, LUTON, MAN CITY, MAN UNITED, NEWCASTLE, NOTTS FOREST, PORTSMOUTH, PRESTON, SHEFFIELD WED

Xmas
2nd Eleven

A slightly more balanced side with slightly more amusing names.

We couldn't find a decent side using real names, so we've resorted to cheap tricks and made some up. Sure, we've still had to use Deco as a right back - but I reckon this lot might score a few goals.

Manager:
Ian Hollaway-in-a-manger

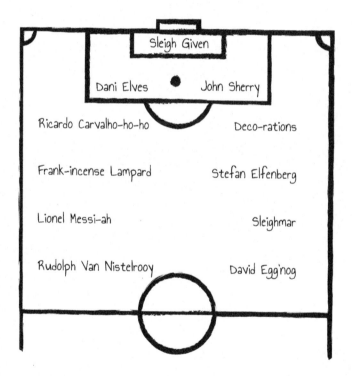

Sleigh Given

Dani Elves   John Sherry

Ricardo Carvalho-ho-ho   Deco-rations

Frank-incense Lampard   Stefan Elfenberg

Lionel Messi-ah   Sleighmar

Rudolph Van Nistelrooy   David Egg'nog

Cracker-attack!

Shhh! It's Cracker Time!

The Fire brigade phones Aston Villa's manager in the early hours of Sunday morning...

"Sorry to inform you sir, but the stadium is on fire!"

"The cups! We have to save the cups!" replies the Villa Manager.

"Don't worry! The fire hasn't reached the canteen yet!"

Happy Birthday
Chris Kamara

He was born on
Christmas Dayyyyyyyy!

Born in Middlesbrough on Christmas Day 1957, Chris Kamara needs no introduction to fans of English football.

He played nearly 800 games, in a career which spanned all four English divisions, and ten different clubs.

He's achieved even greater success as a TV presenter, famed for his enthusiasm and idiosyncratic presenting style. Whether he's telling us that Spurs are 'fighting like beavers', or exclaiming that he simply 'can't believe it', he's never anything but entertaining.

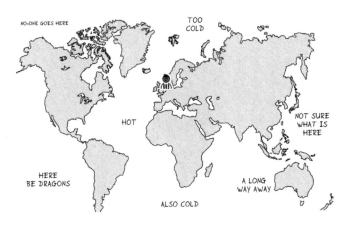

He's usually the presenter 'on the spot' who has to be told from the studio what's happening next to him - his finest moment was failing to spot that a player had been sent off in a match he was reporting on (to be fair he did see him walk off the pitch, but he just thought he was being substituted).

Add in appearances in the Mid Wales League for Welshpool Town (after his Sky Sports colleague Jeff Stelling made fun of them), changing his name to Chris Cabanga due to a Facebook petition (something to do with the World Cup!), and having his own Playstation game (Chris Kamara's Street Soccer) - and you've got a truly memorable Xmas born football superstar!

Fact File

Full name: Christopher Kamara

Known as: Kammy

Nationality: English

Career Caps: 778

Career Goals: 86

Greatest Achievement: It was a tough decision, but we've gone for his Swindon Town player of the year award, from the 1979/80 season.

Last heard of: Entertaining the public as a presenter for Sky Sports.

Name that
Football Club #7

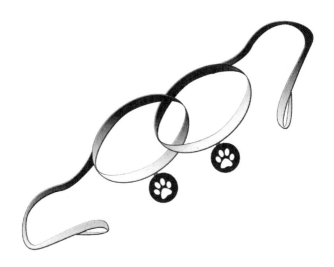

Find the answer at the bottom of page 78.

My Name is...

A quiz about some nicknames that footballer's have.

Harry Kewell, possibly Australia's most skilful footballer ever, was known as The Wizard of Oz. When is the Wizard of Oz on telly? That's right! Christmas! So, without further ado, a quiz about nicknames...

1. Top bearded ginger Alexi Lalas was a US World Cup star, but what drink provides his nickname?

2. Genghis Khan was a fearsome Mongolian leader responsible for fathering thousands of children, and

orphaning many, many more. Which goalkeeper had the 'fortune' to be given the nickname Genghis Khan?

3. Dutch player Ernest Faber must have been handy around the office! Was his nickname The Pencil Sharpener, The Paper Clip or The Stapler?

4. We don't know if Italian World Cup Golden Ball winner Salvatore Schillaci was friends with Harry Kewell, but with his nickname he wouldn't have been out of place in Oz either. What was it?

5. He scored 55 goals for Brazil, and over 700 throughout his career. He's got titles and cup wins galore - and yet his nickname was still Shorty. Who was he?

6. The great Stanley Matthews was known as the Wizard of what?

7. Henri Camara apparently had one of the most unusual nicknames we've ever heard. Was it Smiling Rabbit with a Rifle, or Laughing Rat with a Shotgun?

8. Juan Sebastian Verón may have flopped expensively at Manchester United, but he did have the nickname Brujita. What does it mean? (Clue: If Harry Potter was a lady and he was smaller than he is now, you'd be on the right track!)

Name That Club #7: Leeds United (Leeds)

9. Willy Van de Kerkhof was great to have around if you had a dusty house. What was his nickname?

10. He may not have played for his country, or scored many goals, but he had our favourite ever nickname. What was Fitz Hall known as?

Answers on page 100

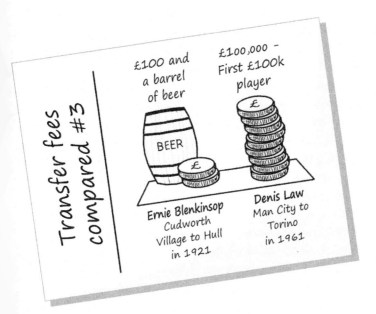

Transfer fees compared #3

£100 and a barrel of beer

£100,000 – First £100k player

BEER

£

£

Ernie Blenkinsop
Cudworth
Village to Hull
in 1921

Denis Law
Man City to
Torino
in 1961

Full Time!
Here are the
Answers!

Please Stop Singing Now

1. Which of these was not a hit for Gazza? 'Fog on the Tyne', 'Howay the Lads' or 'Geordie Boys'? **Howay the Lads**.

2. Which duo known for their classic 80s haircuts (to be fair they did have them in the 80s) caused much pain to our ears with Diamond Lights? **Glenn Hoddle and Chris Waddle.**

3. Andy (Andrew) Cole didn't trouble the charts with his biggest hit. Was it called Amazing, Outstanding, or Fabulous? **Outstanding.**

4. This footballer turned movie 'star' released a cover of the song Big Bad Leroy Brown. Who was he? **Vinnie Jones.**

5. Which German superstar - who played against England in the 1966 World Cup Final and was known as Der Kaiser - once sang 'Gute Freunde Kann Niemand Trennen'? **Franz Beckenbauer.**

6. Which national side tempted fate by calling their 1974 World Cup song 'Back Home'? **England, and they did end up 'back home' a lot earlier than expected!**

7. According to Spurs, whose 'dream' was it to reach Wembley in 1981? **Ossie Ardiles - they released 'Ossie's Dream' on the way to winning the 1981 FA Cup.**

8. Which British national side sang 'Easy, Easy' in 1974? A clue? Their opponents have probably been singing it back to them ever since. **Scotland.**

9. Two comedians and a singer from the Lightning Seeds combined for the song 'Three Lions' in 1996 (and again in 1998 and again in 2010!). You can have an imaginary point for each one you can name. **Ian Broudie, Frank Skinner and David Baddiel.**

10. Lukas Podolski spent eleven weeks in the German top 100 with the single 'Halleluja'. True or False? **True - he featured on the single with German band 'Brings'.**

How Many?

1. Manchester United's record attendance was 83,260 in a game against Arsenal in 1948. Where was the match played? **Man City's ground, Maine Road. Old Trafford was being rebuilt due to damage from the Second World War.**

2. West Ham United's biggest home gate (42,322 against Spurs in 1970) was at the ground many of us know as Upton Park. What is its official name? **The Boleyn Ground.**

3. We've seen that women's football has been played in front of some big crowds in the past - but the record Goodison Park gate was actually broken in 2012, when Britain beat which team 1-0 in the Olympics? **Brazil.**

4. Hampden Park is one of the biggest football grounds in the country, with a capacity of over 52,000. Which club team play their home games there? **Queen's Park (and no, it's not often full!).**

5. Which Brazilian stadium holds the record for the highest ever football attendance – a whopping 199,854! **The Maracanã Stadium (or the Journalist Mário Filho Stadium for the pedants).**

6. Bolton Wanderers played Manchester City in front of nearly seventy thousand fans in a 1933 FA Cup match. What was the name of Bolton's ground in 1933? **Burnden Park.**

7. The largest stadium in world football in 2014 is the Rungnado May Day Stadium. Its capacity is 150,000 and a clue to its location is that attendances are often exactly 150,000. Which country is it in? **North Korea (or the Democratic People's Republic of Korea).**

8. Only one of the five largest football stadiums in the world is in Europe. Whose stadium is it, and what is it called? **Barcelona's Camp Nou stadium.**

9. With a capacity of 120,000 Salt Lake Stadium is one of the largest in world football. Which country is it located in? **India.**

10. The Millennium stadium is Wales' largest football ground. Is its capacity 74,500, 79,500 or 84,500? **74,500.**

Goals, Goals and more Goals

1. On 11th April 2001, American Samoa were beaten 31-0 in a World Cup qualifying match. Which team beat them? Australia. At the end of the match the scoreline actually read 32-0, but after a recount it was reduced to just 31!

2. Two teams with bulging trophy cabinets met in the very first Full Members Cup final in 1986. At the time neither had won a trophy in a decade, but a shiny cup was at stake that day, and a thrilling match ended 5-4. Which teams played in the final? **Manchester City and Chelsea. Chelsea won 5-4, having been 5-1 up with just five minutes to play!**

3. On 12th September 1885, Dundee Harp beat Aberdeen Rovers 35-0 in the Scottish Cup. It would have been a world record; however on the very same day another Scottish Cup game ended 36-0! Who scored 36 goals? Arbroath, Celtic, or Hibernian? **Arbroath.**

4. Ipswich Town (in 1995) and Wigan (in 2009) have both conceded nine goals in Premier League Games. For a point each, name the teams that beat Ipswich and

Wigan. Spurs beat Wigan 9-1 in 2009, while Manchester United beat Ipswich 9-0 in 1995.

5. Poor Wigan improved the next season (2010) - only losing 8-0 to the eventual Champions. Who beat them this time? **Chelsea.**

6. One of the most astonishing World Cup matches took place in 1954 - when one nation, known for its skiing holidays, came back from 3-0 down to beat another nation, also known for its skiing holidays, 7-5. Name the two countries involved. **Switzerland and Austria. Austria won.**

7. Which team, a regular in Europe at the time, recorded their highest ever win (11-0) against Strømsgodset in the 1974 UEFA Cup Winners' Cup? **Liverpool.**

8. Alex Ferguson's last ever game for United was a high scoring draw against West Brom. Was the score 3-3, 4-4 or 5-5? **5-5. The Baggies twice came back from 3 goals down to draw level.**

9. In a 1943 cup game, having lost the away leg 3-0, Real Madrid won the return 11-1. 70 years later it was still their record win. Who did they beat? **Amazingly it was Barcelona. At the time Spain was ruled by the dictator**

Franco and it's fair to say he wasn't a fan of the Catalan team. Barcelona's players were given a message by

Franco's head of security before the match, suggesting that if they won, this might be the last game they played.

10. In 2002 a match in Madagascar ended with a world record 149-0 scoreline. How did the winning team score so many goals? They didn't. The losing side Stade Olympique de l'Emyrne had just lost the championship due to a disputed penalty decision in a drawn game. They used their next match, against AS Adema (who had won the Championship as a result of the disputed dropped points) to protest - and so it was the losing side that scored 149 own goals.

You only sing when you're losing

1. It's 2004. You're playing at home, winning 3-0 at half time in an FA Cup tie. One of your opponent's best players gets sent off DURING the half time break for dissent. You lose 4-3 with the winning goal coming in the 90th minute. You are Spurs - but who were you playing? **Manchester City - Joey Barton got sent off at half time, and Jon Macken scored that winning goal.**

2. Artmedia are from Slovakia - and if you've heard of them, it's probably because you're a fan of the British club they knocked out of the Champions League in 2005. Artmedia won their home leg 5-0 and then clung on to lose by just 4 goals in the away game, against which team? **Celtic. The 5-0 defeat was Gordon Strachan's first competitive match as Celtic manager.**

3. Liverpool were the shock 1-0 losers in the 1988 FA Cup Final. Who beat them, and, for an extra imaginary point, which future Northern Ireland manager scored the winning goal? **Wimbledon won, with Lawrie Sanchez scoring.**

4. France arrived at the 2002 World Cup Finals as World and European Champions. They incredibly lost their first

match 1-0 to an African team that went on to reach the Quarter Finals? Name that team. **Senegal beat France, with Papa Bouba Diop scoring the only goal of the game.**

5. In 1966, Italy were beaten 1-0 in one of the biggest ever World Cup upsets. Italy, twice winners of the trophy, were playing an Asian team who had never previously qualified. Which country beat Italy? **North Korea. They made it through to the quarter finals and even held a 3-0 lead against Portugal, inside thirty minutes. However Portugal fought back and won the game 5-3.**

6. When the Faroe Islands entered qualifying for the 1992 European Championships, they didn't even have a pitch to play on. Their first competitive game was played in Sweden against a team that once finished in third place at a World Cup Finals. The Faroe Islands won 1-0. Who were the big losers that day? **Austria.**

7. Germany don't often get beaten at home. And they would never let one of their biggest rivals score five goals against them in a competitive match - or would they? We all know England beat Germany 5-1 in 2001 - but who scored the goals? **Steven Gerrard and Emile**

Heskey both scored one, and Michael Owen got a hat-trick.

8. Spain were hosting their first World Cup. Fancied to do well, they were leading their group going into the final game of the first stage. They were playing a country with a population just 1/25th the size of Spain. A country who hadn't qualified for over 20 years. They lost the game 1-0. Which team beat them, and who scored the winning goal? **Northern Ireland - Gerry Armstrong scored.**

9. We're back at the 2002 World Cup Finals and once again it's Italy on the end of a shock result. One of the unfancied host nations is playing - surely there can only be one result? Indeed there is, as the Italians lose 2-1 and typically conjure up a host of conspiracy theories. But which team beat them? **What is it with Italy and Korea? This time it was South Korea - and the winning goal was scored by Ahn Jung-hwan who plays in... Italy! At least he did, as the next day his contract with Perugia was cancelled. Ah well, I guess a bad loser is still a loser.**

10. It's only the Capital One Cup - and they were playing a weakened team. But when the new manager of

Manchester United is Louis Van Gaal, and he's spent more than a little cash, you don't expect to lose 4-0 to a team two divisions below. Which team beat United? **MK Dons.**

They Call Him What?!

1. Which Italian, who played for Middlesbrough, was known as The White Feather? **Fabrizio Ravanelli.**

2. Who was the Baby-Faced Assassin? **Ole Gunnar Solskjær.**

3. What was England goalkeeper David James' cowboy themed nickname? **Calamity James.**

4. Which alliterative Frenchman was known as Zizou? **Zinedine Zidane.**

5. Which ex-England manager was known as The Professor? **Fabio Capello.**

6. US footballer Eric Wynalda got his nickname because he liked to dress in striped tops and hide amongst similarly attired gentlemen (at least that's our theory). What was his nickname? **Waldo. (A trick one as Where's Wally is Where's Waldo in the US and Canada).**

7. Javier Zanetti has played over 600 games for Inter, and picked up an unusual nickname along the way. Is he known as The Plough, The Tractor, or The Combine Harvester? **The Tractor.**

8. Why wouldn't you like Givanildo Vieira de Sousa when he's angry? **Because he's the Hulk!**

9. Spanish player Emilio Butragueño, was known as the Vampire. True or False? **False - he was the Vulture.**

10. Which of England's World Cup winning Charlton brothers was known as The Giraffe? **Jack Charlton.**

Oh we do like to be beside the Seaside!

1. Blackpool is clearly the world's finest seaside town, so what better place to start. One of their nicknames is the colour of their shirts - What is it? **The Tangerines (not Oranges).**

2. Alan Shearer scored a whopping 260 Premier League goals - but which seaside club did he start his professional career with? **Southampton.** He scored goals for them too, but they were before the start of the Premier League so Sky and the FA told us that they don't really exist.

3. Which coastal club play at the Liberty Stadium? **Swansea City.**

4. Barcelona are the only seaside team in this quiz who have won the European Cup - but when did they first win it - 1961, 1986 or 1992? **1992. They were beaten finalists in the other two years.**

5. Bournemouth may not have a long list of European titles, but they did win the very first Football League Trophy (then known as the Associate Members' Cup) in 1983-84. Who did they beat in the final? Hull City, Burnley or Millwall? **Hull City - who we wanted to include in this seaside list - but we were overruled by some pedant with knowledge of the Humber estuary.**

6. They famously beat Liverpool with a shot that deflected off a Beach Ball. How seasidey is that? Name the team. **Sunderland.**

7. Which coastal club are known as the Shrimpers? **Southend United.**

8. Which Scottish football club play in the Granite City? Aberdeen. It is known as the Granite City because many of its building are made using granite from a nearby quarry.

9. Portsmouth won the 2008 FA Cup final - but who did they beat? **Cardiff City 1-0.**

10. And an easy one to finish. Which coastal city has a club whose name ends in Argyle? **Plymouth.**

Naughty or Nice?

1. Which fiery Italian was banned for 11 matches in 1998 for pushing over referee Paul Alcock? **Paulo Di Canio - contact was minimal, but the ref was entitled to go down.**

2. Chelsea dumped Adrian Mutu in 2004 after he got in trouble with gambling, women, or drugs? **Drugs. He was banned for seven months for taking cocaine.**

3. In the 2006 World Cup, English referee Graham Poll sent off Josip Šimunić for receiving more than one yellow card. What was unusual, and which team did Šimunić play for? **He played for Croatia, and Graham Poll accidentally gave him THREE yellow cards before sending him off.**

4. This Brazilian, bought by Inter as a teenager for over £10 million, must hold some kind of record for being thrown out of clubs. Amongst other incidents, Inter twice sent him back to Brazil on unpaid leave, São Paulo released him early from a loan after he wandered out of training, Roma terminated his 3 year contract

after just seven months, and Corinthians released him due to an apparent lack of interest in training! Who is he? **Adriano.**

5. Luis Suarez had a nibble of Giorgio Chiellini at the 2014 World Cup - but this wasn't the first time he'd snacked on an opponent, it was the third time! Which club was he playing for when he had his first footballer dinner? **Ajax. He bit PSV's Otman Bakkal in 2010 and was banned for seven matches.**

6. Manchester United's Eric Cantona famously karate kicked an opposition fan who was abusing him. Which club was the fan supporting? **Crystal Palace.**

7. In 2014 Arsenal's Kieran Gibbs was sent off for handball in a match against Chelsea. What was unusual about his dismissal? He had been mistaken for Alex Oxlade-Chamberlain - and despite both players explaining the mistake to the referee, it was Gibbs who had to walk.

8. Maradona crushed England's World Cup hopes in 1986 when he handled the ball into the net. He later called it the 'hand of God' - but who was the England keeper that he tricked? **Peter Shilton. Even though keepers weren't quite the giants they are today, you've got to hand it to the 5'5" Maradona for reaching the ball even with his fist!**

9. Norman Hunter was a classic hard man in that heyday of dodgy tackling, the late 60s/early 70s. But was his nickname Breaks Yer Back, Grinds Yer Gears, or Bites Yer Legs? **It was Bites Yer Legs - a name given to him by the fans at Leeds.**

10. Zinedine Zidane would have been known simply as one of the greatest footballers ever - until he headbutted an opponent in his last ever game, the 2006 World Cup Final. Who did he headbut, and what team did his opponent play for? **Marco Materazzi of Italy.**

My Name is...

1. Top bearded ginger Alexi Lalas was a US World Cup star, but what drink provides his nickname? **Red Bull.**

2. Genghis Khan was a fearsome Mongolian leader responsible for fathering thousands of children, and orphaning many, many more. Which goalkeeper had the 'fortune' to be given the nickname Genghis Khan? **German keeper Oliver Kahn**

3. Dutch player Ernest Faber must have been handy around the office! Was his nickname The Pencil Sharpener, The Paper Clip or The Stapler? **The Paper Clip.**

4. We don't know if Italian World Cup Golden Ball winner Salvatore Schillaci was friends with Harry Kewell, but with his nickname he wouldn't have been out of place in Oz either. What was it? **Toto - Toto was the name of the dog in the Wizard of Oz (but he wasn't named after the dog).**

5. He scored 55 goals for Brazil, and over 700 throughout his career. He's got titles and cup wins galore - and yet his nickname was still Shorty. Who was he? **Romario.**

6. The great Stanley Matthews was known as the Wizard of what? **Dribble.**

7. Henri Camara apparently had one of the most unusual nicknames we've ever heard. Was it Smiling Rabbit with a Rifle, or Laughing Rat with a Shotgun? **Smiling Rabbit with a Rifle.**

8. Juan Sebastian Verón may have flopped expensively at Manchester United, but he did have the nickname Brujita. What does it mean? (Clue: If Harry Potter was a lady and he was smaller than he is now, you'd be on the right track!) **Little Witch!**

9. Willy Van de Kerkhof was great to have around if you had a dusty house. What was his nickname? **The Vacuum Cleaner**

10. He may not have played for his country, or scored many goals, but he had our favourite ever nickname. What was Fitz Hall known as? **One Size (not sure why? Think about it...think some more... say his nickname then his name... Now?)**

Anagram Answers – Mixed up Stadiums

1. Hampden Park (Queen's Park and Scotland)

2. Stamford Bridge (Chelsea)

3. Anfield (Liverpool)

4. Vale Park (Port Vale)

5. Racecourse Ground (Wrexham)

6. Alexandra Stadium (Crewe Alexandra)

7. The Shay (Halifax)

8. New York Stadium (Rotherham United)

9. Selhurst Park (Crystal Palace)

Answer- Xmas Comes Early

1. Gordon Banks

2. George Cohen

3. Jack Charlton

4. Bobby Moore

5. Ray Wilson

6. Nobby Stiles

7. Alan Ball

8. Bobby Charlton

9. Martin Peters

10. Geoff Hurst

11. Roger Hunt

If your brain was as big as a football - The Solution

Which player will reach the Quarter Finals? *Gary Boots*

Who will travel by Bicycle? *Joey Jump*

Who plays as a Winger? *Gary Boots*

	Qualifying	Group	Qtr Final	Semi Final	Final	Goalkeeper	Right Back	Ctr Midfield	Winger	Striker	Ferrari	Bicycle	Bentley	Porsche	Walks
Gary Boots	✗	✗	✓	✗	✗	✗	✗	✗	✓	✗	✗	✗	✓	✗	✗
Claudio Kicko	✗	✓	✗	✗	✗	✗	✗	✗	✗	✓	✗	✗	✗	✗	✓
Billy Ball	✗	✗	✗	✓	✗	✗	✓	✗	✗	✗	✗	✗	✗	✓	✗
Joey Jump	✓	✗	✗	✗	✗	✗	✗	✓	✗	✗	✗	✓	✗	✗	✗
Goalinho	✗	✗	✗	✗	✓	✓	✗	✗	✗	✗	✓	✗	✗	✗	✗
Ferrari	✗	✗	✗	✗	✓	✓	✗	✗	✗	✗					
Bicycle	✓	✗	✗	✗	✗	✗	✗	✓	✗	✗					
Bentley	✗	✗	✓	✗	✗	✗	✗	✗	✓	✗					
Porsche	✗	✗	✗	✓	✗	✗	✓	✗	✗	✗					
Walks	✗	✓	✗	✗	✗	✗	✗	✗	✗	✓					
Goalkeeper	✗	✗	✗	✗	✓										
Right Back	✗	✗	✗	✓	✗										
Ctr Midfield	✓	✗	✗	✗	✗										
Winger	✗	✗	✓	✗	✗										
Striker	✗	✓	✗	✗	✗										

Anagram Answers –
Mixed up Players

1. Steven Gerrard

2. Alexis Sanchez

3. Pele

4. Gareth Bale

5. Mario Balotelli

6. Arjen Robben

7. Robert Lewandowski

8. Andrea Pirlo

9. Bobby Moore

They Scored on Boxing Day!

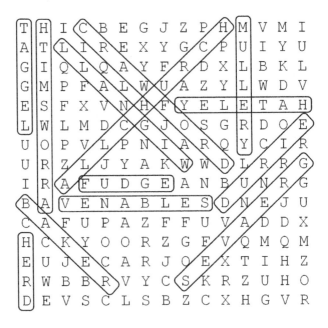

Anagram Answers – Mixed up Teams

1. Nottingham Forest

2. Huddersfield Town

3. Wolverhampton Wanderers

4. Sheffield Wednesday

5. Arsenal

6. Portsmouth

7. Doncaster Rovers

8. Bayern Munich

9. Plymouth Argyle

Answers - Spot the difference

Answers: Capital A in title; String missing from hanging ball; Extra hanging ball added; Tongue on opposite side; Short sleeves; Black section missing from ball on tree; Extra snowflake; Extra laces on boots; Extra ribbon on present.

Match the stadium to the team

Hillsborough Stadium............................Sheffield Wednesday

Elland Road...Leeds United

Riverside Stadium...Middlesbrough

Ricoh Arena..Coventry City

Portman Road...Ipswich Town

Stadium of Light...Sunderland

Molineux.. Wolverhampton Wanderers

St Andrew's...Birmingham City

Valley Parade...Bradford City

They played on Xmas Day!

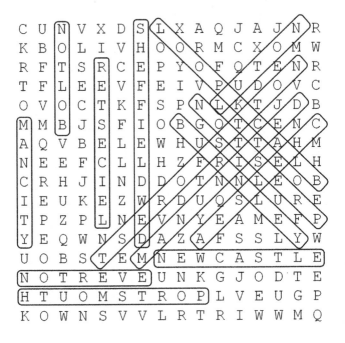

Match the player to the country

Ahmed Hassan...Egypt

Mohamed Al-Deayea...Saudi Arabia

Claudio Suárez ....Mexico

Iván Hurtado ....Ecuador

Iker Casillas...Spain

Vitālijs Astafjevs...Latvia

Cobi Jones..United States

Adnan Al-Talyani...............................United Arab Emirates

Martin Reim..Estonia

Printed in Great Britain
by Amazon